T0417665

FANtastic Franchises

TEENAGE MUTANT NINJA TURTLES FRANCHISE

Kenny Abdo

Fly!
An Imprint of Abdo Zoom
abdobooks.com

abdobooks.com

Published by Abdo Zoom, a division of ABDO, P.O. Box 398166, Minneapolis, Minnesota 55439.

Printed in the United States of America, North Mankato, Minnesota.
052024
092024

Photo Credits: Alamy, Everett Collection, Getty Images, Shutterstock, ©National Museum of American History p10, p11 / CC0 1.0 Universal
Production Contributors: Kenny Abdo, Jennie Forsberg, Grace Hansen
Design Contributors: Candice Keimig, Neil Klinepier, Colleen McLaren

Library of Congress Control Number: 2023948524

Publisher's Cataloging-in-Publication Data

Names: Abdo, Kenny, author.
Title: Teenage Mutant Ninja Turtles franchise / by Kenny Abdo
Description: Minneapolis, Minnesota : Abdo Zoom, 2025 | Series: FANtastic franchises | Includes online resources and index.
Identifiers: ISBN 9781098285616 (lib. bdg.) | ISBN 9781098286316 (ebook) | ISBN 9781098286668 (Read-to-me eBook)
Subjects: LCSH: Mirage Studios, Inc.--Juvenile literature. | Teenage Mutant Ninja Turtles (Series)--Juvenile literature. | Teenage Mutant Ninja Turtles (Fictitious characters)--Juvenile literature. | Turtles--Juvenile literature. | Branding (Marketing)--Juvenile literature. | Popular culture--Juvenile literature.
Classification: DDC 338.768--dc23

TABLE OF CONTENTS

TEENAGE MUTANT NINJA TURTLES

From comic book pages to the big screen, the crime-fighting Teenage Mutant Ninja Turtles (TMNT) have brought fans of all ages out of their shells!

ORIGINS

SEAL OF THE STATE OF NEW HAMPSHIRE
1776
CREATION OF THE
TEENAGE MUTANT NINJA TURTLES
In November 1983, while living in Dover, Kevin Eastman and Peter Laird created a cast of Ninja weapon-wielding turtles during a late-night drawing session. Amused by the absurdity of the idea, the duo developed the story of four teenage turtle brothers: Leonardo, Raphael, Donatello and Michelangelo. The one-shot comic, published independently by Mirage Studios on Union Street, debuted in 1984. Teenage Mutant Ninja Turtles soon became a full comic series and ultimately an international multimedia franchise.
2023

Artists Kevin Eastman and Peter Laird came up with TMNT in 1983. Eastman drew a turtle standing up, wearing a mask, and holding nunchucks as a joke. He wrote "Ninja Turtle" above it.

Laird outlined the picture and added three more turtles. The two began **fleshing out** the idea for a comic book. But the shelled heroes needed names.

Michelangelo

Raphael

They looked to famous Italian artists for **inspiration**. Finally, the world was ready to meet Michelangelo, Raphael, Donatello, and Leonardo.

THROUGH THE YEARS

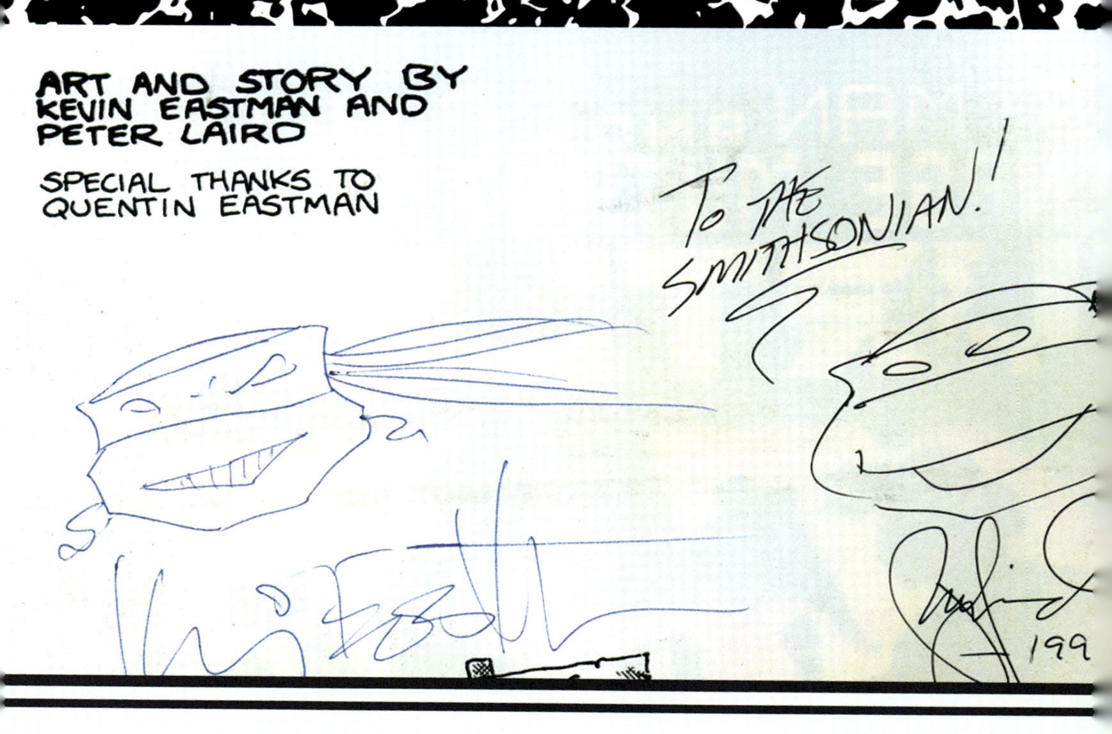

Eastman and Laird opened Mirage Studios in 1984. They used their own money and a loan from Eastman's uncle. Just 3,000 copies of *Teenage Mutant Ninja Turtles* were printed.

Meant to be a **one-shot**, the comic sold out immediately! So, Eastman and Laird began working on a series. Sales continued to grow with each issue that was released.

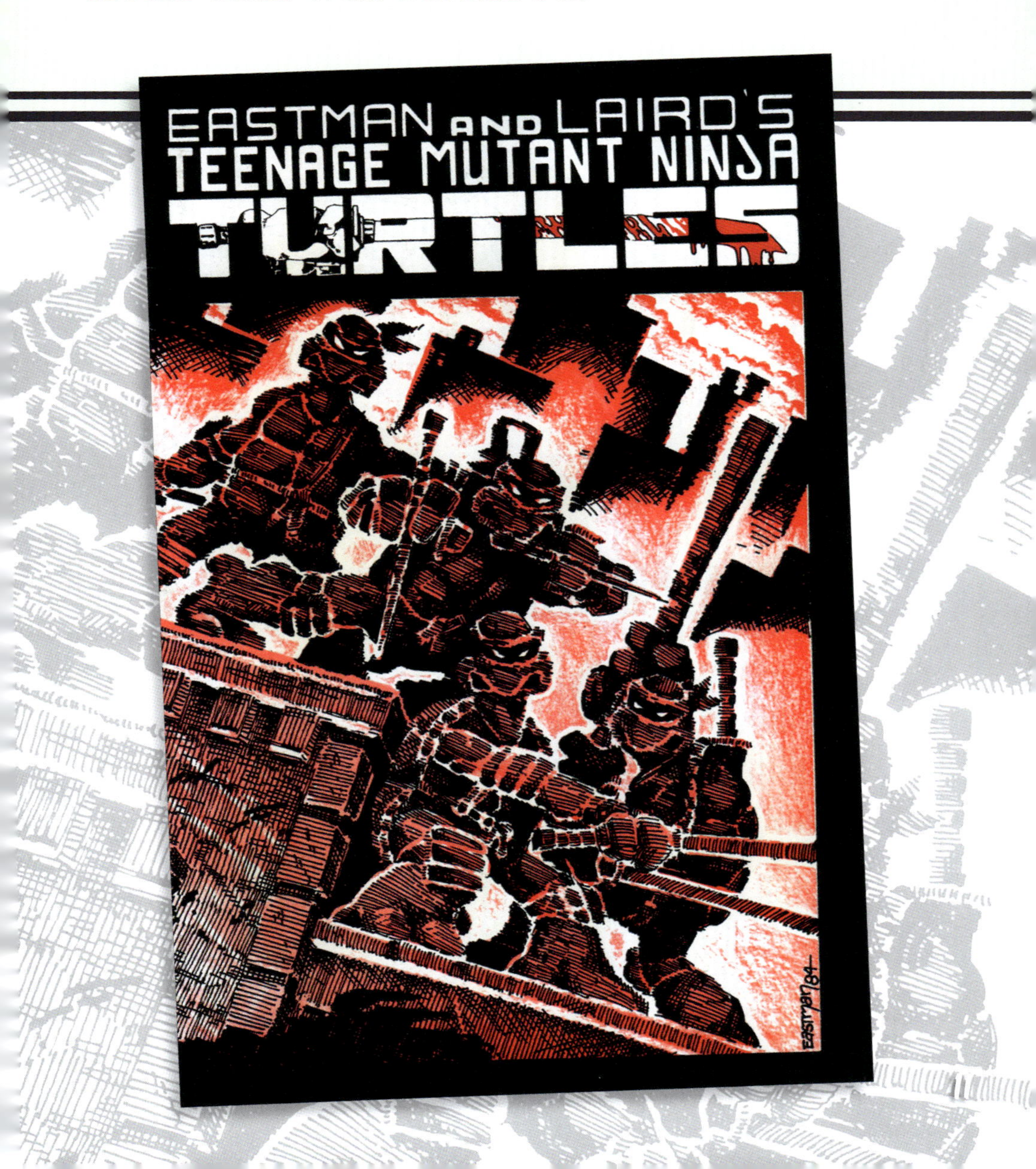

In 1987, the company Playmates Toys **licensed** TMNT. The toys became even more popular than the comics! More than $1 billion of toys were sold in four years.

TEENAGE MUTANT HERO
TEENAGE MUTANT NINJA
TURTLES
Pizza Power Game
GIANT
30

Playmates Toys hired an animation studio to create a TMNT cartoon. The show was meant to promote the toys. However, *Teenage Mutant Ninja Turtles* grew a loyal fan base. The show aired for ten years!

A **live-action** movie was released in 1990. Muppets creator Jim Henson brought the turtles to life using foam latex. *Teenage Mutant Ninja Turtles* became the highest-**grossing** independent film of all time!

Two **sequels** quickly followed the first film. However, they were not as successful. Turtle-mania began to slow down. A few more animated shows were made. In 2009, Laird sold TMNT to Nickelodeon.

Another **live-action** TMNT movie was released in 2014. It did well at the box-office. The **sequel**, *Out of the Shadows*, followed in 2016. Eastman even had a **cameo** as a pizza delivery guy!

Turtle-mania was revived in 2023! The animated movie *Mutant Mayhem* was a huge hit. The unique animation and humor introduced a new, younger audience to the Ninja Turtles!

FANDOM

The Turtles' reach goes beyond just comics and movies. The team has been featured in video games, concert tours, and even roller coaster rides!

What started as a joke between two artists became a **franchise** that gathered a crazed fan base around the world. And TMNT remains **iconic** because they are "turtley" awesome!

GLOSSARY

cameo – a brief appearance of a well-known person in a movie.

fleshing out – making something more complete by adding details.

franchise – a collection of related movies, TV Shows, and other media in a series.

grossing – earning.

iconic – widely known or easily recognized.

inspiration – to gain motivation or creativity from another source.

license – permission granted by an artist or creator to allow another business to use their work.

live-action – involving real, traditional actors and cameras.

one-shot – a comic book story told in just one issue.

sequel – a movie or other work that continues the story begun in an earlier work.

ONLINE RESOURCES

To learn more about the Teenage Mutant Ninja Turtles franchise, please visit **abdobooklinks.com** or scan this QR code. These links are routinely monitored and updated to provide the most current information available.

INDEX